the language of
promise

an interactive journal

book six

being with God series

the language of promise

We are called to inherit. The love language of God is vital to that discovery.

Graham Cooke

Brilliant Book House

Brilliant Book House
6391 Leisure Town Road
Vacaville, California 95687
USA
www.brilliantbookhouse.com

Requests for information regarding Graham's ministry should be addressed to:
Graham Cooke
Future Training Institute
6391 Leisure Town Road
Vacaville, California
USA
office@grahamcooke.com
www.grahamcooke.com

ISBN 978-1-934-771-07-5

dedication

I dedicate this journal to all the friends, ministry supporters and prayer partners who have sustained Heather and me through many years of warfare, work, pain and challenge.

Thanks for being true, committed and faithful. May you inherit every blessing that the Father has planned and purposed for your lives. Jesus deserves a people full of confidence in the promises He lavishes upon them.

acknowledgments

I want to thank the journal team of Carole Shiers (my personal assistant), Tim Pettingale (my friend and publisher) and his staff at Sovereign World, and Jordan and Jenny Bateman (editorial). They are a great bunch to work with on a project close to my heart.

Their tireless work, enthusiasm, and unflagging good humour have helped to make this project one of life's great pleasures.

Together, we are all learning the language of promise.

introduction

Jesus was getting used to operating under the critical eye of the Sadducees and Pharisees. He had encountered them many times in His ministry and had always used the beauty of God's truth to stay one step ahead of them. Today would be no different. The Pharisees had heard that Jesus had stumped the Sadducees, so one of them, a lawyer, asked Him a loaded question: "Teacher, which is the great commandment in the law?"

Jesus' answer summed up the call on every Christian who has followed Him in the 2,000 years since. *"The first of all the commandments is: 'Hear, O Israel, the Lord our God, the Lord is one. And you shall love the Lord your God with all your heart, with all your soul, with all your mind, and with all your strength.' This is the first commandment. And the second, like it, is this: 'You shall love your neighbor as yourself.' There is no other commandment greater than these,"* Jesus replied in Mark 12:29–31. Christianity can be boiled down into those two statements: our role in life is to love God, and to love everyone we come into contact with.

Jesus has not asked us to do something He has not already done Himself. God always obeys His own word – He cannot go against His own decrees. He does not ask us to do something He would not do Himself. We can therefore look at the first commandment and know that He loves us with all of His heart, all of His soul, all of His mind, and all of His strength.

Never doubt that you are absolutely and completely loved by God. You are His beloved. Your role in life is to receive that love, return it to Him, and pass it along to everyone around you. It's a tough job, I know, but someone's got to do it. Love Him with everything in you – it all belongs to Him, anyway. And love anyone you come into contact with; anyone within touching distance. It doesn't matter what you're doing, where you're going, or who you're meeting – you are called to love others. It is irrelevant whether they are Christian or pre-Christian; they are your neighbours and you are called to touch them with the love of God.

God has taken the lead in this. He has come to each and every one of us and poured His love into our spirits: *I love you with all of My heart, all of My soul, all of My mind, and all of My strength. Everything in Me is dedicated to loving you. I've poured this love into you and you're going to have the pleasure of giving it back to Me.*

This is our greatest blessing: we are loved passionately by God.

Graham Cooke
August 2003

the language of promise

Love is a topic that has been explored, pondered, considered, and written about for as long as humans have been around. It has been looked at from almost every angle, and is an experiential common ground for humanity: everyone understands the feeling of love. Many, however, have a distorted view of the power of love. They have tried to capture it without seeking out its origin, God.

The Apostle John understood well where love originated. *"We love because He first loved us,"* he wrote in 1 John 4:19. Before we were saved, most of us were going through life completely oblivious to who God really is. One day, suddenly and miraculously, God invaded our world; taking the initiative and reaching out to us in love. We responded by returning that love to Him, and found ourselves walking in salvation.

The way that we begin life in God is the same way that life continues with Him. God took the initial step: He loved us first. He came looking for us, spoke to us, sent those weird people to share the gospel with us. We looked at those strange people that were sent into our lives and thought, "Wow, they seem a bit out of step with the real world." But there was something that drew us: God Himself.

Our relationship with God is sustained by the same force of love by which it was birthed. God doesn't stop taking the initiative the moment we are saved. He is continually our Lover, and we are continually His beloved. Our job is to be loved by God: only God can love God. He comes into our lives and fills them with hope, faith, and love. That pure love does something inside of us which we give back to Him.

> "Life is to be fortified by many friendships. To love and to be loved is the greatest happiness of existence."
> Sydney Smith

God's language is love

God adores us because He wants our adoration. God loves us because He wants our love. God speaks to us by His love. This is the language we need to hear from the Lord so that we can speak it back to Him. It's a glorious cycle – God takes the initiative by loving us, and we return that love to Him. God can say nothing without using this language of love.

notes

notes

notes

notes

What is true in the natural is also true by the Spirit. Isaiah described this beautifully in 55:9–11 (NASB):

For as the heavens are higher than the earth,
So are My ways higher than your ways
And My thoughts than your thoughts.

For as the rain and the snow come down from
     heaven,
And do not return there without watering the earth
And making it bear and sprout,
And furnishing seed to the sower and bread to the
     eater;

So will My word be which goes forth from My
     mouth;
It will not return to Me empty,
Without accomplishing what I desire,
*And without succeeding **in the matter** for which I*
     sent it.

God's promise is as inevitable as rain falling, His words water our lives, making us fruitful and productive. We return this blessing through our words of praise and thanksgiving, our testimony and witness to His Nature and also by our actions that may bring glory to the Lord.

James put it a different way, but it is still the same theme:

Every good thing given and every perfect gift is from above, coming down from the Father of lights, with whom there is no variation or shifting shadow. In the exercise of His will He brought us forth by the word of truth, so that we would be a kind of first fruits among His creatures.

(James 1:17–18 NASB)

Everything that is good and right comes from a Father who never changes. It is His consistency and faithfulness that is the bedrock of our ability to receive. It simply does not depend upon us! He is the origin, the cause, the motive and the source of every gift. It will always be this way. He is the Beginning and the Ending for all of us, for all time. His passion is to make each of us a joyful carrier of His word through His promises so that we may enjoy the certainty of our receiving His gifts and goodness.

Think of it: we are the first fruits of His huge desire to have a people represent His Excellence. Our role in the earth is to proclaim the fact of God's outstanding goodness by living the life of promise that He has set aside for us. All God's promises are yes! and amen! in Christ Jesus. Paul put it this way in his letter to the church in Rome:

> *. . . who has first given to Him that it might be paid back to Him again?*

For from Him and through Him and to Him are all things. To Him be the glory forever. Amen.
(Romans 11:35–36 NASB)

It is not possible for us to initiate anything to God. Paul asks who has ever given to God first. God initiates, we respond by receiving and then we give back to God the very thing He gave us in the first place. From, through and to Him are all things. Everything He wants from us He gives to us.

This is amazing, wonderful, outrageous and mind-boggling stuff! This means that when the Holy Spirit convicts me of something, He is also relaying the Father's willingness to supply what I lack. Therefore:

▶ Conviction regarding our inability to pray also released the promise that He will help us.

▶ Struggling with unclean thoughts? Conviction also brings with it the promise of purity.

▶ Problems with doubt, unbelief? With conviction the Lord seeks to initiate faith.

Get the message? The promise releases the gift. Conviction seeks to re-establish the divine order. The Holy Spirit points out our need and the provision at the same time. Conviction restores us to being open to the goodness of God. From Him, through Him and to Him are all things … marvelous.

Each of us must see ourselves in that cycle in the manner that the Father has declared. To live as part of His cycle of life we must understand that all of His language to us is full of promise to us. He delights to speak to us and is blessed by our expectancy.

The tragedy of modern Christianity is that much of it is performance-oriented. We think we have to do something to get something from God. "God can't possibly like me because I'm not doing anything," we say. "God can't love me, I don't pray enough. I don't give enough. I don't worship enough. I don't read enough." But how much is actually enough? We shouldn't be constantly quantifying "enough," but we should be serving God because He loves us. Present-day Christians are quick to fall into the same trap Martha did in Luke 10, thinking that we have to prove ourselves worthy of a relationship with Jesus. Being Mary, and basking in Jesus' love, is a severe challenge for us.

The language of love is something we must all learn. We have to understand how God sees us, so that we can see Him more clearly. God loves us and, because He loves us, we want to talk to Him. Everything we can give to God comes from Him in the first place. It begins and ends with God, because intimacy is a cycle.

"Love is but the discovery of ourselves in others, and the delight in the recognition."
Alexander Smith

In the natural world, we see many examples of this type of cycle. Water falls from the sky, and returns to the heavens by the process of evaporation. The moon does not generate its own light, but reflects the light of the sun in the night sky. The image in a mirror is nothing more than a reflection of the actual object. Likewise, our love for God is a reflection of His love for us. Love begins and ends with God.

We cannot love God on our own initiative, but we can give back that which He has bestowed on us. When the Father of Lights gives us a gift that touches our heart, it does something inside of us. We end up returning to God the very thing He has given us. To love God, we must be loved by God. It's a wonderful thing to go through our entire lives being loved by God. We are condemned to be loved by Him forever. We can't escape it. We have no alternative but to put up with it: this is who God is.

Parents know an example of this principle. When our children were growing up, and our birthday was approaching, most of us gave them money to buy us a present. How do we know how to do this? It is in our DNA. God is the same way; His love is the currency He gives us so that we can love Him more fully. He gives to us the very thing He wants from us!

possessed by God

God chose us so that He could be Himself with us. He wants us to see Him as He really is, and to fall in love with Him the same way He has fallen in love with us. In our relationship, we must come to a place of mutual declaration, as He and the Israelites did in Deuteronomy 26:16–19 (NIV):

> *The LORD your God commands you this day to follow these decrees and laws; carefully observe them with all your heart and with all your soul.*
>
> *You have declared this day that the LORD is your God and that you will walk in his ways, that you will keep his decrees, commands and laws, and that you will obey him.*
>
> *And the LORD has declared this day that you are his people, his treasured possession as he promised, and that you are to keep all his commands. He has declared that he will set you in praise, fame and honor high above all the nations he has made and that you will be a people holy to the LORD your God, as he promised.*

God declared to the Israelites His laws, and they, in return, declared that they would follow them. It was a breakthrough moment for Israel. Just outside of the Promised Land, with their leader, Moses, winding down his life, they finally came to a point of mutual declaration with God. This passage actually fulfilled a prophetic conversation Moses and God had shared forty years earlier, in Exodus 19:3–6:

And Moses went up to God, and the LORD called to him from the mountain, saying, "Thus you shall say to the house of Jacob, and tell the children of Israel: 'You have seen what I did to the Egyptians, and how I bore you on eagles' wings and brought you to Myself. Now therefore, if you will indeed obey My voice and keep My covenant, then you shall be a special treasure to Me above all people; for all the earth is Mine. And you shall be to Me a kingdom of priests and a holy nation.' These are the words which you shall speak to the children of Israel."

Moses and Israel had been out of Egypt for just three months when God spoke these words. The words "special treasure" can also be interpreted as "possession": "If you will indeed obey My voice and keep My covenant, then you shall be *My possession*," God was saying. "The whole earth is Mine, but you will be My special treasure." Those simple words began a prophetic theme from the heart of God which has echoed through countless generations.

This original prophetic blessing was updated and expanded in Deuteronomy 7:6–9:

For you are a holy people to the LORD your God; the LORD your God has chosen you to be a people for Himself, a special treasure above all the peoples on the face of the earth. The LORD did not set His love on you nor choose you because you were more in number than any other people, for you were the least of all peoples; but because the LORD loves you, and because He would keep the oath which He swore to your fathers, the LORD has brought you out with a mighty hand, and redeemed you from the house of bondage, from the hand of Pharaoh king of Egypt. Therefore know that the LORD your God, He is God, the faithful God who keeps covenant and mercy for a thousand generations with those who love Him and keep His commandments.

We have been chosen as God's special treasure not because of who we are, but because of who God is. His love cuts away all of our performance-oriented mentality. God chose you because of who He is; He chose you because of what He is like. You weren't chosen because you are deserving or clever or brilliant or handsome or noble or even good. He chose you because *He* is good. Out of His love and His promises, you were selected as His treasure. God's faithfulness has been the bedrock of His dealings with humanity throughout time. God cannot change – He cannot be anything other than who He is.

"Everybody can be great ... because anybody can serve. You don't have to have a college degree to serve. You don't have to make your subject and verb agree to serve. You only need a heart full of grace, a soul generated by love."
Dr. Martin Luther King, Jr.

Cohabitation with God

Much of the terminology surrounding revival is geared to events and special circumstances. It is largely "visitation" terminology. We are looking for God to come in a move of the Spirit. Yet the language of Scripture is one of abiding, a habitation of the Spirit being built inside each of us.

In reality, revival is not about large numbers of people discovering the King and His kingdom. Something that is dead spiritually cannot be revived, it must be born again. Revival is for the church, not the world. We must wake up from our sleep.

Revival has three stages. First is renewal of our passion for Jesus; we must return to our first love and learn to be abandoned to His grace and power. Secondly we must be revived in our compassion for the lost; to give our lives in service of the kingdom. The outcome of these two initiatives will release the final stage reformation where the world will begin to respond to the power and the glory of a risen Lord, inhabiting His people.

We need to lay down our agendas and words and give ourselves, day in and day out, to loving Jesus. *"He who believes in Me, as the Scripture has said, out of his heart will flow rivers of living water,"* Jesus taught in John 7:38. People all too often come to church meetings because they are thirsty. I just cannot understand that. We should be coming to meetings because we're full of water and wanting to give some more of it away.

Learning to cohabit with God takes time. The pressure of ministry is intense: it can stress us out, make us sick, even kill us, unless we know how to rest in the Lord. It takes discipline to bring ourselves to a place of peace before God, but it is absolutely necessary to do so. It has taken years of practice for me, but, on most days, I can bring myself to that place of peace in five or ten seconds. It no longer matters what is swirling around me or threatening me, I can still myself before God. I have to: I need to be quiet to hear His voice. God loves to speak in whispers. He rarely answers prayers at the same decibel level at which they are prayed.

"Father!" we can shout at Him. "I need to hear Your voice!"

"I know," He whispers back.

"Speak to me," we bellow at the top of our lungs.

"I am," He whispers.

"I need to hear Your voice today!" we blare.

"Shut up and listen," He whispers.

"Be still, and know that I am God," says Psalm 46:10. Meditation is another avenue towards cohabitation with God. The western church must learn to meditate, setting time aside to think deeply about God. It doesn't have to be long: just fifteen minutes or

half-an-hour, but the more you do it, the more time you'll want to give to Him. I love meditating.

Meditation and stillness flow into an upgrade of our peace. I spend a lot of time on peace with the people I disciple. I constantly confront them on the issue of peace in their lives. I don't expect them to worry or panic at the same level next year as they did this year. Their peace must increase, and anxiety decrease. Peace is a vital fruit of the Spirit.

Without an upgrade in our capacity to rest in the Lord, we find ourselves running on adrenaline. That's okay for a while, but for every adrenaline high, there's an adrenaline low. Often, people get down and depressed because they have been running on adrenaline, and they've run out. It's not the pressure of life that gets to us, it's the pressure of how we run it.

Peace, though, is an equalizing pressure. If the world is throwing a thousand pounds of pressure at you from the outside, peace sends a thousand and one pounds from the inside. I'm under pressure wherever I go – intense pressure in most places. Everyone wants to see me and talk to me and pull at me and get prayer from me. I don't mind; it's my job. To survive, I have learned to be at peace. My rest in God gives me space.

> "If the world is throwing a thousand pounds of pressure at you from the outside, peace sends a thousand and one pounds from the inside."

Eventually, adrenaline will rob our mind and body and will leave us exhausted. It's okay to be tired *in* the work, but it's not okay to be tired *of* the work. We must learn to give ourselves to peace, rest, and meditation. We can operate at the highest level for many years if we have developed ourselves internally in preparation.

sonship and stewardship

We live our lives in the tension of a paradox between *being* and *doing.* The key to succeeding in this quandary is to always choose *being* over *doing.* We must choose to take time out to rest. We all have to do many things, but being is just as important. This paradox could be described as the difference between *sonship* and *stewardship.* We must learn how to serve the Lord but we must also explore how to be a son of God. God doesn't want to treat you like a slave – He wants to treat you like a son.

One of my mentors, Arthur, once asked me, "Graham, do you want to be a servant of the Lord?"

"Yes," I answered.

"Then don't get upset if He treats you like one," Arthur said.

Sometimes, God commands and I obey. Other times, He makes a request of me because He wants to treat me like His son. Christians need to know how to live life as both a servant and a son. Being a son means God gets the best of our day, not just the tail end. The Apostle Paul is a wonderful example of a man who knew how to be both a servant and a son, as we read in Ephesians 1:15–23:

Therefore I also, after I heard of your faith in the Lord Jesus and your love for all the saints, do not cease to give thanks for you, making mention of you in my prayers: that the God of our Lord Jesus Christ, the Father of glory, may give to you the spirit of wisdom and revelation in the knowledge of Him, the eyes of your understanding being enlightened; that you may know what is the hope of His calling, what are the riches of the glory of His inheritance in the saints, and what is the exceeding greatness of His power toward us who believe, according to the working of His mighty power which He worked in Christ when He raised Him from the dead and seated Him at His right hand in the heavenly places, far above all principality and power and might and dominion, and every name that is named, not only in this age but also in that which is to come.

And He put all things under His feet, and gave Him to be head over all things to the church, which is His body, the fullness of Him who fills all in all.

What an incredible prayer! Longevity in the spirit is powered by wisdom and revelation from God. The two streams flow into one, enabling us to understand who God wants to be for us. Once we capture who God wants to be for us, there is a power and energy that flows into our spirit from His own. Suddenly, we're living life for all it's worth. Defeats and burnout evaporate. A Spirit-infused Christian does not become weary or overwhelmed by circumstances because his or her eyes are lightened with the knowledge of who God is. His call on our lives is certain.

Living in the Spirit gives us a glimpse of the riches of our inheritance. God loves to show us His majesty and power so that in every situation we face, we can rely on Him. *"I know whom I have believed and am persuaded that He is able to keep what I have committed to Him,"* Paul wrote his young charge Timothy in 2 Timothy 1:12. He had absolute confidence in who God was for him: his deliverer, his protector, his passion. Paul was able to go into places where incredible opposition swirled because he knew God was with him. He was always himself, and spoke the words of God to kings and vagabonds.

> "Two roads diverged in a wood, and I ... I took the one less traveled by, and that has made all the difference."
> Robert Frost

Each of us can only go as far as God has given us permission to go. Our authority grows as our maturity in Christ grows. By knowing who God is for us, we never have to be afraid of our circumstances.

lessons from Ephesus and two women

The paradox of being and doing is seen throughout Scripture. In Revelation 2:1–5, we see one example of this phenomenon, in a letter written by Christ to the church at Ephesus:

To the angel of the church of Ephesus write,

"These things says He who holds the seven stars in His right hand, who walks in the midst of the seven golden lampstands: 'I know your works, your labor, your patience, and that you cannot bear those who are evil. And you have tested those who say they are apostles and are not, and have found them liars; and you have persevered and have patience, and have labored for My name's sake and have not become weary. Nevertheless I have this against you, that you have left your first love. Remember therefore from where you have fallen; repent and do the first works, or else I will come to you quickly and remove your lampstand from its place – unless you repent.'"

The church of Ephesus was full of good, hardworking people. They loved to *do* ministry. Their church endured and persevered through troubles. They were efficient and did good deeds. Yet somehow their relationship with God had gotten lost in all of the business. *"I have this against you, that you have left your first love,"* Jesus said. *"Remember therefore from where you have fallen; repent and do the first works."* In other words, God was calling Ephesus to think back to its acts of adoration and to reconnect with Him in worship.

Repentance means to change one's mind and find a different paradigm to live under. Ephesus, and by extension all Christians who *do* more than *be*, needed to change its lifestyle to reflect its most urgent priority: worshiping God. *"Do the first works"* – start by practicing all of the things you used to do in praise, in worship, and in your devotional life.

God doesn't actually need people to evangelize the earth, do missions projects, or give away millions of dollars. What He is looking for are people who will worship Him in spirit and in truth. That doesn't just mean singing in meetings, or going for it when the band is rocking. He wants people who worship Him in the way they live. He wants people like Mary and Martha, as recorded in Luke 10:38–42:

> *Now it happened as they went that He entered a certain village; and a certain woman named Martha welcomed Him into her house. And she had a sister called Mary, who also sat at Jesus' feet and heard His word. But Martha was distracted with much serving, and she approached Him and said,*

"Lord, do You not care that my sister has left me to serve alone? Therefore tell her to help me."

And Jesus answered and said to her, "Martha, Martha, you are worried and troubled about many things. But one thing is needed, and Mary has chosen that good part, which will not be taken away from her."

Both Mary and Martha were right, but for completely different reasons. Paradoxes aren't about one right answer and one wrong one: both sides of a paradox are right. The issue is primacy. When push comes to shove, what is most important to us? What takes precedence? Without Martha's, very little would get done in the Church. Martha's sacrifice, organize and create places where Mary's can flourish in worship. But without Mary's, everything we do would come from a religious duty. We actually need both. Each one of us is a Mary and a Martha, and both are legitimate. One of them has precedence, and that's Mary. Mary is where we receive insight into the things God has placed inside of us.

> "Each one of us is a Mary and a Martha, and both are legitimate."

Jesus Christ: treasure hunter

Throughout His earthly ministry, Jesus spoke to the treasure God had deposited in people. He even blessed the spiritual treasure that the person themselves did not realize they had. In Luke 19, Jesus met a crooked tax collector named Zacchaeus. Not once did Jesus reveal the man's sin. All He did was bless him and honour him. Humbled, Zacchaeus knew what to do: "Look, Lord, I give half of my goods to the poor; and if I have taken anything from anyone by false accusation, I restore fourfold." The man simply stopped cheating others, signed away half of his possessions, and made a contract with Heaven to restore what he had previously stolen. "I robbed you of a hundred dollars; here's four hundred back" – that's God at work in one of His special treasures.

God has placed His fingerprint in the people around us, and we need to speak to that spiritual treasure. In John 1, the disciple Philip brought his brother, Nathanael, to meet Jesus. Nathanael, at first, was skeptical: *"Can anything good come out of Nazareth?"* he asked. But when he finally met Jesus, the Lord spoke to the treasure in him: *"Behold, an Israelite indeed, in whom is no deceit,"* Jesus said, noting that He had prophetically seen Nathanael sitting under a fig tree earlier that day. *"Rabbi, You are the Son of God! You are the King of Israel,"* exclaimed Nathanael, who left everything behind and became a disciple. Jesus had spotted the treasure – that piece of God's Spirit that had been deposited in Nathanael's life – and spoken to it. Nathanael, in turn, became a pillar of the early Church.

speak to the treasure

Jesus knew that whatever He spoke to would rise up in people. Humanity always speaks to the earthen vessel, noting every crack, flaw, and warp: "If you put this right, and change that, then we'll let you in and accept you." God is not remotely like that. He speaks to the treasure in a person and releases it from the captivity of the flesh. He extracts the precious from the worthless. We often try and do the opposite; we take out the trash and see what's left. When we speak to the treasure in people, it moves to the surface of their lives, from the hidden to the obvious. The rubbish always comes with it. When people see their own worth, they get rid of their own carnality. That's why the prophetic and the pastoral go so well together. But God knows there is treasure in each of us and He want to bring it to the surface. Don't let your view of the worthless obscure that which is precious about a person.

We have got to change the way we think of, and behave around, other people. We don't have any enemies except for the devil and his demons. The Apostle Paul believed this: *"For we do not wrestle against flesh and blood, but against principalities, against powers, against the rulers of the darkness of this age, against spiritual hosts of wickedness in the heavenly places,"* he wrote in Ephesians 6:12. We don't have any human enemies, only people who we are not finding the treasure in. Fortunately, God can give us a different type of vision to help us see people in a new way.

"Let it be the hidden person of the heart, with the incorruptible beauty of a gentle and quiet spirit, which is very precious in the sight of God," Peter wrote in 1 Peter 3:4. "Incorruptible" in this verse means that the beauty will not pass away; unlike a flower that blooms and withers, that which is precious in God's eyes stands forever. When God looks at you, He see what is precious – what He most loves about you right now.

> "I have found the paradox that if I love until it hurts, then there is no hurt, but only more love."
> Mother Teresa

love your enemy

Christians are so quick to demonize other believers; unfortunately, I have witnessed many examples of this fact. I remember talking with a well-known church leader whose associate pastor, after many years, had left and started another church five miles down the road.

"I discipled this guy for fifteen years and he went and left me!" the leader told me. "He's got an Absalom spirit!"

"What does that look like?" I asked.

"You know, Absalom. He's a traitor," the leader

replied. "He's taken what is mine and seized it for himself."

I was surprised by the conversation. "I know that man," I said. "And the truth is that he can only be an Absalom if you have been a David. If you have been fatherly to him, kingly, looked after him, loved him, and wanted only to see him succeed, then, yes, he is an Absalom. But if you haven't done that, he can't be an Absalom."

After a few moments of silence, I continued on. "You know what, he might be a Jacob and you might be a Laban. Did you ever think about that? It works both ways."

He frowned at me, but I pressed ahead. "You're not seeing things clearly," I said. "Maybe you have forgotten all of the years that he served you. Maybe you have forgotten his faithfulness, like the time the church was having financial troubles and he took a pay cut so you wouldn't have to. Maybe you have forgotten to see what God has put inside of him. Maybe he just feels that he has only one life and he needs to live it. You got so used to him serving you that you forgot to serve him. You're a good man, and you can see this for yourself. In your heart, you are a father, and you've just missed that point for a few moments. Why don't you go down the road and say to him, 'How can I help you be successful?' You could lend him some of your people for a while, or see if he

You see

I see a mountain, you see a miracle
I see a wasteland, you see a garden
I see dry bones, you see an army
I see the impossible, you see everything

I see a seed, you see a harvest
I see the water, you see the wine
I see the broken, you see your body
I see my enemy, you see your footstool.

> You are, I am
> But I've been so blind, all this time
> My God, touch me
> I want to see the way that you see

I see my sins, you see your blood
I see a baby, you see my saviour
I see my failures, you see redemption
I see a beggar, you see a son

I see a problem, you see a provision
I see a crisis, you see an opportunity
I see the image, you see the heart
I see opposition, you see someone to love

> You are, I am
> But I've been so blind, all this time
> My God, touch me
> I want to see the way that you see

I see the weary, you see the warriors
I see the restless, you see their peace
I see the doubting, you see their faith
I see the weak, you see their strength

I see my Father, you see your son
I see my Shepherd, you see your lamb
I see my Saviour, you see your joy
I see your eyes, staring into mine

> You are, I am
> But I've been so blind, all this time
> My God, touch me
> I want to see the way that you see

Inspired by the lyrics of Jonathon Helser
a songwriter, worshiper, catalyst and
a man after God's own heart.

is okay financially. You might want to get behind him on some evangelistic initiatives just to bless him. Maybe you could just let him know that, even though he has a problem or two, you see the good in him. Knowing you, you'll probably want to do all of this and more, because you are a godly guy."

The leader paused and looked at me. "Do you want a coffee?" he asked. I got the message: *Subject closed.*

> "Hatred paralyzes life; love releases it. Hatred confuses life; love harmonizes it. Hatred darkens life; love illumines it."
>
> Dr. Martin Luther King, Jr.

Some time later, the former associate called me and told me that he and the leader had gotten together for coffee. He had apologized and had began paying half of the man's salary, and sent teams to help him with the church plant.

"What happened?" the former associate asked me, completely bewildered.

"I think he just saw the treasure in you, because God showed him the treasure inside of himself," I answered.

start with yourself

Sometimes it's not the quality of their sonship but our fathering that is more the issue. It is not just their commitment to service, but also our capacity to inspire and disciple. These things always work both ways. Getting God's perspective first enables us to position our own heart in the Spirit.

That leader had to have a vision for himself – that he was a father, not a slave-owner – before he could have eyes to see the treasure in someone else. When we see ourselves as God sees us, we automatically start seeing others differently. I look at some people and think, "It's in there somewhere – just keep looking, Grae." I want to love people enough to tell them what their treasure is. I don't want to focus on what they're doing against me. I want to come back, in the opposite spirit, and say, "You know something? This is what God likes about you."

This approach confounds people: it's so cool to see. People come to me and say, "I don't like this about you, or this, or this." I just smile, look at them, and reply: "You're probably right, because I am less than perfect. But you know, this is what God likes about you. God loves this part of you! Let me just bless that in you, so you can get stronger." It's called heaping coals of fire on their head, and it's a lot of fun. They usually leave bewildered by the conversation, but touched by the Spirit.

Some of us have had our minds so damaged by others that we simply believe we are worthless. I curse that thought in the name of Jesus: that is not God. We should each know our value and worth to the Lord. It's not based on what we have done, but on who He is. Our doings will catch up with our being – don't fret about that. But God loves you, right now, just as you are. He will continue to change and form you, because He is kind, generous, and in love with you.

In the Bible, God compared us with pure gold:

> *The precious sons of Zion,*
> *Valuable as fine gold,*
> *How they are regarded as clay pots,*
> *The work of the hands of the potter!"*
>
> (Lamentations 4:2)

People see us as just another clay pot, made by a potter's hand; but God sees us as fine gold. Sometimes we can't see the spiritual beauty in a person because of the earthen vessel, but it is there. And whatever you see in people that is good, or speak to people that is good, rebounds on you. God judges every idle word, and blesses every precious one.

> "God loves you, right now, just as you are."

what you are and what you aren't

Everything we do is both an *act of worship* and an *act of war*. A good day's work is an act of worship because it demonstrates something about the Kingdom of God. It's also an act of war because the enemy hates employment. Spending time with God is a powerful act of worship, and a terrifying act of war: our intimacy with the Lord intimidates the demonic. Every word of praise, every word of thanksgiving, and every thought of adoration is a salvo in the battle against evil.

The enemy hates thankful people and enjoys misery. He loves grief, sadness, unhappiness, low self-esteem, and anything that keeps a human from connecting with God. The Spirit of Christ is put into humans to ward those feelings off – God wants us to know how He feels about us. In that knowledge He then wants us to reach out and take the grave clothes from off the people around us. Everything positive and good is a spirit contribution that attacks death and decay, bringing light, hope and warmth into someone's heart.

My personality has never lent itself well to the stage. I'm very much an introvert, so what you see in my preaching is completely fueled by God's anointing. I love the way God made me. Andreas Hermann, a German friend of mine, once said that "introverts have a very colourful inner life." He was absolutely correct. I do have a colourful inner life.

The downside of being introverted is that I get overwhelmed by myself some days. Waves of thoughts about what I am not crash over me, leaving me overwhelmed. Those thoughts are easily overcome, however. I need only think of how God feels about me – His love and adoration and kindness for me – and those worried thoughts dissipate. I'm not fooled by myself. I know what I'm like without Jesus, but I also know what my potential in Him is.

"And He said to me, 'My grace is sufficient for you, for My strength is made perfect in weakness.' Therefore most gladly I will rather boast in my infirmities, that the power of Christ may rest upon me. Therefore I take pleasure in infirmities, in reproaches, in needs, in persecutions, in distresses, for Christ's sake. For when I am weak, then I am strong," Paul wrote in 2 Corinthians 12:9–10. Christians can look at God and thank Him for our deficiencies. He covers all of those weaknesses.

It's okay to come to God and say, "I don't deserve to be here. I'm only here by Your grace, Your goodness, Your mercy, and Your overwhelming kindness." I often tell the Lord that I don't know why He chose me, except that He must be looking for someone slow and degenerate. I fit that bill! Every Christian lives their life by the grace of God. Our deficiencies are more than made up for by the Holy Spirit. God can and will make up the shortfall in our life. God stands in our credibility gap and smiles. He stands in our hypocrisy and gives us legitimacy. And He does it gladly!

God calls each of us as a Jacob and makes us an Israel. This is the transition that each of us will work through all the days of our life. In that space between Jacob and Israel stands Jesus Himself, loving us and offering us His credibility. This love is why Christians should be the most grateful people on the face of the earth.

We need to return to the right spiritual disciplines because our prime goal must be to remain in the presence of God. We need to believe in the power and ministry of the Holy Spirit to sustain a devotional lifestyle. These disciplines – blessing, prayer, meditation, peace, rest, worship, thanksgiving, and praise – are God's language of promise.

> "Only believe."
> Smith Wigglesworth

The Holy Spirit is committed to seeing you connect with God no matter what state your life is in. His job is to help you find and enjoy the grace of God. The Lord loved you when He saw the worst you had ever been. In fact, what you are not endears you to Him. God came and chose and loved you in the midst of all of your sin, hypocrisy, inadequacy, and inability. And as He works in your life, your ability to experience that non-negotiable love is increasing. His love never changes, but the way we receive it does. It is we that grow, not Him.

To our minds, it seems like God loves us more now than He did before. This is untrue. What has changed is that we believed His love, say, ten percent back then, and we believe it twenty-three percent now. Next year, we might believe forty-five percent of His love. Eventually, one day, we're going to believe all of the love God has for us. At that moment, nothing on earth will be able to stop us from becoming the person God has called us to be. Through the leading of the Holy Spirit, our confidence and faith in the nature of God can reach the same level and dimension of His love for us.

bless, bless, and bless some more

If we were really sensible, we would be out there, blessing up a storm, because every blessing we give someone returns to us. I write, on average, twenty cards a week. I should have bought shares in Hallmark. I'll sit and think about people and ask the Lord to tell me something about them. God then shows me something precious and I write.

> "The love we give away is the only love we keep."
> Elbert Hubbard

Sometimes, it's just a few sentences: "I was thinking about you today and this is what the Lord told me about you. Just thought you might want to know."

I do this, and it seems to returns to me tenfold. I remember being at home one day when Carole, my personal assistant, called to ask how I was doing.

"Really good," I answered.

She laughed and said, "Well, Graham, we've got thirty-five cards in the office for you. Are you sure you're not struggling with anything?"

"Actually, yes, I am struggling with something," I sighed. "I've been praying for it but I don't know how I feel about it. I'm on the edge of it: I still feel good about myself, but something's up." I went to the office and read the thirty-five cards, and twenty-seven of them spoke encouragement in the very issue I was facing.

You can't sow potatoes and reap rhubarb. To be blessed and encouraged, we must bless and encourage others.

living by faith

I am never in need of encouragement or money because all I want to do is give both away. I have learned to hold on to both loosely, living by faith. I don't have a salary: I prefer to live by faith.

My struggles early on in the ministry to live by faith were centered mainly around my inability to rest. I had not worked out that the Father not only provides, but also stretches our faith at the same time. That often meant the provision was delayed (my terminology) or at least never showed up when I was at the limit of my faith. However, it seems that God disagreed about where my limit was and so each situation took me beyond my previous measure.

In the gap between promise and provision I was slowly learning that I had choices to make. Either I

notes

notes

notes

could rest in God's language of promise ("My God shall supply all your need in Christ Jesus"), or I could try to make things happen by dropping hints to people, sending out prayer letters, expending my own efforts. Often in that hiatus I would get irritable and impatient with people around, usually Heather.

I was not only learning about faith and how it grows by stretching, I was also discovering that faith must be undergirded by peace. In Paul's letter to the Hebrews, chapter 4, Paul unites faith and rest: we who have believed enter that peace.

He wrote about labouring to enter a place of peace and calmness. Rest has to be worked at constantly or faith will whither. Everyone must increase their peace levels to be able to stay in the war, live the life and move in the supernatural.

Our faith is in the nature of God. It is not about faith in faith. So often I have heard people say that they didn't have enough faith. It is not the size of our faith that is important, but the depth of our revelation of God's nature. When we know what He is really like, when our hearts are emboldened by the majesty of His faithfulness and grace, then we know that His commitment to His word and His people cannot be broken. His word will not return to Him empty.

Faith is driven by what we have seen, heard and experienced of the true nature of the Father. Our faith always pushes out beyond our experience; it never

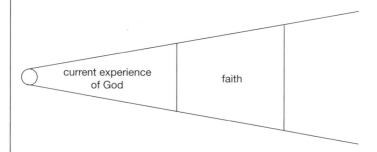

Figure 1

stays at the same place. Our current experience helps us to believe God more at the next opportunity (see Figure 1). That's what Scripture means when it says we walk by faith, not sight.

There is always a dimension where faith is beyond our experience. Faith is exploring, pushing us beyond the boundaries of what we know in the natural. As we get used to that faith level, our experience pushes up to it and our faith ranges out further into the heart of God (see Figure 2).

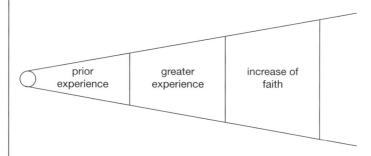

Figure 2

Shoes

My child, walk in My footsteps, live in My shoes.
This is your place of safety because I am bigger than anything or
anyone you will ever face.

This is your place of provision, for you will walk in My increase for
your life.
This is your place of expansion for I am growing you to fit the
anointing that I have set aside for you.

You have power to stand in Me.
My strength is yours as you walk in Me.
Walking in bloody footsteps, your sins are forgiven and your
weaknesses are covered.

Enjoy this life.
Be a child in Me.
Speak to your enemy, your detractors, your problems with the same
confident word…
"My God is bigger that you".

It will always and ever, be True!

Our faith is always in advance of our experience, so that we always have something to aim for in the nature of God. In the storm on the lake (Mark 4), the disciples had faith in their own seamanship but not in Jesus' power to control the elements. Faith gave out and fear came in as a result. The size of faith is always a lesser issue than where it is placed.

real prosperity

In Acts 10:9–16, the Apostle Peter had a vision that changed the course of church history:

> *The next day, as they went on their journey and drew near the city, Peter went up on the housetop to pray, about the sixth hour. Then he became very hungry and wanted to eat; but while they made ready, he fell into a trance and saw heaven opened and an object like a great sheet bound at the four corners, descending to him and let down to the earth. In it were all kinds of four-footed animals of the earth, wild beasts, creeping things, and birds of the air. And a voice came to him, "Rise, Peter; kill and eat."*
>
> *But Peter said, "Not so, Lord! For I have never eaten anything common or unclean."*
>
> *And a voice spoke to him again the second time, "What God has cleansed you must not call*

common." This was done three times. And the object was taken up into heaven again.

God wanted Peter to see people the way He sees them – as precious treasures. "Don't call them dirty, Peter, I love them." The real prosperity message is *"Christ in you, the hope of glory"* (Colossians 1:27). We must look for Jesus in the people around us. God has sent us on a treasure hunt to find what He has implanted in people.

> "Love in its essence is spiritual fire."
> Emanuel Swedenborg

In the beginning, God said, *"Let Us make man in Our image, according to Our likeness"* (Genesis 1:26). We must search for the image of God in every human being, looking for what is precious in Christian and pre-Christian alike.

a devotional lifestyle

Our search for the treasure in other people is just one part of the devotional lifestyle needed to free our ministry from stress and worry.

One of my earliest mentors once said to me, "You have to be in ministry for about twenty or twenty-five years before God will trust you with your life's message. In the first twenty years, everything is training and preparation for what God truly wants you to do." That's why longevity is so important in ministry. We must learn to live in a place where we can run without growing tired. We have to replenish ourselves in the Spirit every day.

Successful ministers plan for the future but live for today. They place their lives in day-tight compartments, taking everything one day at a time. At the end of a day, they know how to shrug everything off, cleanse their hearts and minds, and be thankful for the blessings God has given them. When they awake the next morning, they awake anew to the tangible mercies of God. Those mercies are like a first cup of coffee or a first mouthful of food.

When I first started out in prophetic ministry nearly thirty years ago, there were six of us in England. There were probably more like 6,000 prophetic ministers, but I only knew six – and half of them were weird. On some days I didn't know which group I belonged to! Ministry is relentless on people:

▶ a quarter of all prophets have nervous breakdowns

▶ sixty percent of all pastors quit leading churches

▶ fifty percent of the people leaving the ministry do so because of immorality

▶ another thirty percent leave because of stress

Behind most of these statistics is a rundown devotional life. When we lose our focus on God, we end up with a working relationship – but a lousy friendship – with Him. The only way a lot of ministers relate with

God is on the basis of what they do for Him. Everything is business when someone has lost their devotional life. We end up praying about ministry: the youth group, Sunday School, finances, consumed by the business of ministry and not the joy of friendship with the Father.

> "We have become so engrossed in the work of the Lord that we have forgotten the Lord of the work."
> A.W. Tozer

I wonder how many of us have upgraded our ability to praise and thank God in the past twelve months. We need to praise God more this year than we did last year. Many of us take time out every day to pray, but how many of us take time to just adore Jesus? There are a few questions which we can ask that will help us get to the heart of the matter:

- ▶ What currently attracts you to Jesus?
- ▶ What draws you to Him right now?
- ▶ What aspect of His nature overwhelms you in His presence?
- ▶ What is the most important thing for you to recover in your relationship with God?
- ▶ What gift does the Lord long to give you?

idolatry

A sixth question could be added to that list:

- ▶ What currently distracts you from enjoying the presence of God?

Martha was pulled away from Jesus' presence by her sense of duty and by the work necessary to house a guest of Jesus' stature. What interests you most has taken a piece of your heart. If the combination of people and things in your heart is greater than your love for God, your spirituality will hit a ceiling and level off. Often we do not know where God is in our life because we have not given Him much room to move. The clutter of our other loves and desires, legitimate though some may be, can prevent His reality from being expressed. In extreme cases, they can even shut Him out all together.

Many Christians are lukewarm in their fellowship with the Lord because the balance of their love and attention is swung away from the Father. Idolatry has such a beginning.

His love raises the water table of all our other affections: it's as if our love for others comes up ten levels because of how we feel about Him. When God rules out of your absolute love for Him, all other loves improve and increase.

> "Without worship,
> we go about miserable."
> A.W. Tozer

Whatever comes between God and us is an idol. Whether it's our leadership, career, business, ministry, family, or anything else, it's an idol. At that point, we are headed for either a pruning or a serious chastisement because God is a jealous God. He will not have anything come between He and His children. Take some time and make sure your life is in proportion.

Jesus' words to the church in Ephesus need to ring loud and clear in our spirits: *"Remember therefore from where you have fallen; repent and do the first works, or else I will come to you quickly and remove your lampstand from its place – unless you repent."* The lampstand represents the place of revelation, influence, and ministry – a beacon of light to ourselves and others. God must have preeminence.

true worship

At the beginning of our spiritual journey, none of us know the adventures God has in store. We can't really comprehend who we're called to be in His Kingdom. To discover our place, we must seek out wisdom and revelation from God. Without an intimate relationship with Him, we'll never find our way. Our inheritance will pass us by; our future may be something other than we could have realized.

To move out of our inadequacies and into a significant place in the Kingdom, we must allow the Holy Spirit to work in our life. The Spirit will help us upgrade our worship, praise and adoration. When we learn to worship in spirit and in truth, as Jesus implored us to in John 4:23 – 24, we will see ourselves in a way we have never experienced before.

Worship attracts this revelation. When we get into a place of worship, we start to discover things that God wants us to know. Scales fall off of our eyes, and our minds are renewed. We begin to have dreams, see visions, and have thoughts so profound that we have to write them down.

> "Worship is God's enjoyment of us and our enjoyment of Him. Worship is a response to the Father—child relationship."
> Graham Hendrick

In Ephesians 1, Paul prayed that we would have *"the spirit of wisdom and revelation in the knowledge of Him."* This knowledge is all about what God wants to be for us. This revelation gives us energy and peace; it overcomes who we are.

When I'm overwhelmed, I'm always rescued by the same spirit of wisdom and revelation about who God is for me. I get out of the trap of my inadequacy and insecurity by remembering everything He has done for me. In our weakness, He comes and kisses us and calls us again.

gratitude

Gratefulness may be humanity's most underestimated devotional tool. We often forget that gratitude is how we access God's presence. *"Enter into His gates with thanksgiving and into His courts with praise. Be thankful to Him, and bless His name. For the LORD is good; His mercy is everlasting, and His truth endures to all generations,"* the psalmist sang in Psalm 100:4–5.

It's always good to set aside a few hours just to be thankful. Make a list of the things you're grateful for. A lack of gratitude can lead us into feeling that nothing is happening, or into frustration over hassles and issues. In that moment, stop and ask yourself: "What are the benefits in my life right now?"

In the west, we don't know how well-off we truly are. Two-thirds of the world doesn't eat more than five meals a week. God has blessed us and it's important that we think about it. I long to see Christians get beyond themselves and start seeing the glory of God as it pertains to their own life. We need great people who understand that their success is wrapped up in the sovereignty of God.

> "If you concentrate on finding whatever is good in every situation, you will discover that your life will suddenly be filled with gratitude, a feeling that nurtures the soul."
> Rabbi Harold Kushner

If we can do that, a faith, power, energy and zeal will emerge that will take us forward in the things of the Holy Spirit. We must become overwhelmed with who God wants to be for us.

inheriting the promise

And we desire that each one of you show the same diligence so as to realize the full assurance of hope until the end, so that you will not be sluggish, but imitators of those who through faith and patience inherit the promises. For when God made the

notes

notes

notes

promise to Abraham, since He could swear by no one greater, He swore by Himself, saying, "I WILL SURLEY BLESS YOU, AND I WILL SURLEY MULTIPLY YOU." And so, having patiently waited, he obtained the promise.

For men swear by one greater than themselves, and with them an oath given as confirmation is an end of every dispute. In the same way God, desiring even more to show to the heirs of the promise the unchangeableness of His purpose, interposed with an oath, so that by two unchangeable things in which it is impossible for God to lie, we who have taken refuge would have strong encouragement to take hold of hope set before us. This hope we have as an anchor of the soul, a hope both sure and steadfast and one which enters within the veil, where Jesus has entered as a forerunner for us, having become a high priest forever according to the order of Melchizedek. (Hebrews 6:11–20 NASB)

At the heart of all God's dealings with us, is the issue of our inheritance in Christ. We are the Beloved of the Father, the Bride of Christ, People of the Spirit.

not returning evil for evil or insult for insult, but giving a blessing instead; for you were called for the very purpose that you might inherit a blessing.
(1 Peter 3:9 NASB)

We are called to inherit. It is what we demonstrate to the earth. We are people of promise. We have hope, an inheritance and a language in which we communicate our confidence in the Father. That language we learn from heaven. The Holy Spirit communicates the heart of the Father in such a powerful way that we are radically changed by the conversation and the content. We then communicate to others in exactly the way that we heard it from the Lord. Same intonation, the same breathless excitement, the exact same confidence boosting manner in which it was delivered to our heart.

To inherit we need two priceless things which we receive from God in the process of our circumstances. These are faith and patience. This is a wonderful contrast that is only learned through process. Process is a series of steps designed to achieve a particular goal or learning objective.

Faith speaks about immediacy and patience refers to eventuality. Most Christians want the magic Midas touch of instantaneous receiving from the Lord. Faith is a gift to be received but also a disciplined confidence that must be learned. We cannot go through life always requiring a gift of faith. God gives those as He wills. He wants us to learn how to grow faith, increase in it and walk by it. For this to occur we must attach patience to our faith so that we walk on the path that God has provided. Circumstances are often so intense that they seem to last for ages. Primarily this is because we face them in our emotion rather than our will. The will is the vehicle for faith to attain the will of God.

The promise is secure. God does not lie. The issue is always process. The path of God (process) is always about increasing our confidence, enlarging expectation, learning to stand in peace, being stretched in faith and being schooled in how to see God and hold onto Him. His word is the anchor point for process to be attained.

What is the gap between the promise and the provision for you in your current situation? What is the process that is designed to fit that space? What is the pathway that God has chosen for you to develop greater confidence as well as receive the provision? Mediate on these things and activate your will towards the Lord. Learn what your current process is all about and how you can co-operate with the Spirit. This is walking by faith.

Faith is confident expectation, patience is calmness and composure. The two combined produce a fortitude and consistency. There is a serene persistence that allows us to keep God in our sights and rejoice in Him. Serene persistence is anathema to doubt, fear and unbelief.

God is unchanging and trustworthy, so is His word. When promising Abraham a son, the Father took an oath in His own name. The oath and God's name are the same. God's name and His nature are equally the same. Because of Who He is, our confident expectation (hope) is anchored in His personality.

His promises emanate from behind the curtain i.e. the division that separates the Holy Place from the Most Holy Place. This is the place Jesus occupies as our High Priest. He is in God's Presence at all times, continuously interceding for us to be all that the Father intends.

The promise may be fulfilled immediately because the Lord may be showing you how to handle a gift of faith. The promise will always be fulfilled eventually through the process of faith.

Give yourself to the Father of lights, from whom every gift is given (James 1:17). He is the Unchanging One. We see Him best when we are single minded (focus) about His goodness. Double-minded people are always disappointed and eventually disinherit themselves.

Process is the key to walking by faith. Actively combining your faith with patience gives a guarantee of inheritance. Serene persistence ... there is nothing more precious in a faith lifestyle.

conclusion

The sad truth about many longtime Christians is that they have never understood the magnitude of God's love. Some have served Him for decades and not known His passion for them. But I believe that He is going to make up for that lost time. We need to receive this love with a child-like simplicity, not overanalyzing it or trying to strive for it.

God is going to come to us in this next season of time and His love will almost be beyond our capacity to bear. It will be the stuff of dreams, an unimaginable, monumental, incredible, astonishing, marvelous, outrageous love. This language will change the way you think about everything. God's dream for us is that we would be immersed in the majesty of everything He feels for us.

His love will overwhelm us, leading us past logic, reason, intellect, and into a place where our hearts will be touched as they have never been touched before. This is a season of wonder for us, and we will have to learn to live like a much-loved child.

Our journey now is to cultivate an expectancy for – and interpret everything in – the love of God. God wants to root and ground us in His love so deeply that we live there for the rest of our days. This love will cause us to grow to be the men and women God most wants us to be.

It's exciting to think of how radically this love will change our lives. We will experience the breadth, length, height, and depth of God's love for us. His language will wash over us, again and again.

Love God and love our neighbour: it is our destiny and our honour.

notes

meditation

To meditate means to think deeply about something or someone. It means to explore with mind and heart, allowing what you think to touch your innermost being.

Meditation is creative thought which leads us to the higher realm of revelation and wisdom. It takes us beyond the place of reason to where joy is seated and faith is activated.

Meditation allows us to search inside and outside the box of our current paradigm. What you see and hear there touches you profoundly. It adds a ring around the core truth of Christ which is God within, the certainty of freedom.

Fruitful meditation is therefore not a casual seeking for revelatory insight. Initial creative thoughts are merely the X that marks the spot. There is treasure in meditation, a guarantee of wealth in the pursuit of God.

Many are satisfied with collecting random truth on the surface of their consciousness. It is good wholesome stuff but it does not satisfy and it cannot challenge the complexities of life in a warfare context.

Deep truth has to be mined over days and weeks. It takes joy and patience to take truth down to its deepest level. Beyond meeting our current needs. Beyond the depth of understanding the power it releases to us against our adversary. Down to the depth where God lives in the highest places of heaven. For all meditation must ultimately come before the throne of His majesty, sovereignty and supremacy. He fills all things with Himself.

Our current situation requires wisdom, but even more it yearns for Presence. Meditation allows us to experience both, through the word coming alive in our spirit. Meditation leads us to God and the permission of His heart. Learn to be in the question peacefully with God. Let the Holy Spirit teach you how to abide. Turn inwardly and rest, wait patiently ... He will come. When your heart gets restless turn to worship. When the interior atmosphere settles return to listening.

Write down initial thoughts but do not pursue them just yet. Do not be distracted by what you hear initially. Set it aside, come back to it later.

When first entering a lifestyle of mediation, take care to ease into it slowly. An hour at first, then longer until half a day and so on.

Always have a focus, do not try to wait in a vacuum. In this next exercise is a particular statement, followed by a series of questions. This is both to give you practice in meditation and to bring you into revelation of God through the focus statement.

Use the questions as the Spirit leads. This exercise is

not prescriptive but merely a guide to enable your contemplation. No doubt you will discover better questions as the Holy Spirit tutors you. Enjoy!

notes

meditation exercise

" ... stand in your problem, holding onto the promise, looking for the provision."

▶ Engage your heart with the picture this statement provokes.

▶ What does this mean for you?

▶ What problems currently require God's blessing?

▶ What particular promise is the Holy Spirit drawing to your attention? Ask for scriptural support.

▶ Study the promise(s). Look for key words and phrases. Write down specifically what the Lord is guaranteeing to you in your current circumstances.

▶ How will you stand and position yourself before the Father?

▶ What level of confidence does the Father wish to bestow upon you?

▶ What fear, unbelief and inadequacy must you give up in favour of the promise?

► View the promise and the provision together until they fill your vision and hope/faith begin to rise.

► Now, through the lens of the promise, look at the problem. What has changed in your:
  – heart?
  – viewpoint?
  – mindset?

► Compose a prayer before the Lord, a request for His grace, kindness and power to enable you to receive.

► Write a psalm of thanksgiving to the Lord for what He has done in and for you in this current situation.

► Write out in full a confession and a declaration that you can speak into your circumstances by the power of the Holy Spirit.

► As you challenge your circumstances with your newfound revelation a boldness and confidence will enter your speech. How did you feel?

► Continue declaring, believing and challenging daily until God speaks further or the problem disappears.

► What has changed in you?

► What have you learned?

▶ What have you become in Christ?

▶ Finally, enter all these things in your journal. Keep a record of you walk with God in this way not only to encourage you in later times but also as a legacy to your family and friends.

notes

lectio divina

Lectio Divina (Latin for *Divine Reading*) is an ancient way of reading the Bible – allowing a quiet and contemplative way of coming to God's Word. Lectio Divina opens the pulse of the Scripture, helping readers dig far deeper into the Word than normally happens in a quick glance-over.

In this exercise, we will look at a portion of Scripture and use a modified Lectio Divina technique to engage it. This technique can be used on any piece of Scripture; I highly recommend using it for key Bible passages that the Lord has highlighted for you, and for anything you think might be an inheritance word for your life (see the *Crafted Prayer interactive journal* for more on inheritance words).

> *But now, thus says the LORD, who created you,*
> *O Jacob,*
> *And He who formed you, O Israel:*
> *"Fear not, for I have redeemed you;*
> *I have called you by your name;*
> *You are Mine.*
> *When you pass through the waters, I will be with*
> *you;*

And through the rivers, they shall not overflow you.
When you walk through the fire, you shall not be
    burned,
Nor shall the flame scorch you.
For I am the Lord your God,
The Holy One of Israel, your Saviour;
I gave Egypt for your ransom,
Ethiopia and Seba in your place.
Since you were precious in My sight,
You have been honored,
And I have loved you;
Therefore I will give men for you,
And people for your life.
Fear not, for I am with you;
I will bring your descendants from the east,
And gather you from the west;
I will say to the north, 'Give them up!'
And to the south, 'Do not keep them back!'
Bring My sons from afar,
And My daughters from the ends of the earth –
Everyone who is called by My name,
Whom I have crated for My glory;
I have formed him, yes, I have made him.''

(Isaiah 43:1–7)

1.   Find a place of stillness before God. Embrace His
    peace. Calm your body, breathe slowly ... clear
    your mind of the distractions of life. Ask God to

reveal His rest to you. Whisper the word, "Stillness." This can take some time, but once you're in that place of rest, enjoy it. Worship God out of it.

2. Read the passage twice, slowly.

   a. Allow its words to become familiar to you, sink into your spirit. Picture the scene – become part of it. Listen for pieces that catch your attention.

   b. Following the reading, meditate upon what you have heard. What stands out? Write it down:

. . . .
. . . .
. . . .
. . . .

   c. If a word or phase from the passage seems highlighted to you, write it down:

. . . .

3. Read the passage twice again.

   a. Like waves crashing onto a shore, let the words of the scrpiture crash onto your spirit. What are you discerning? What are you hearing? What are you feeling? Write it down:

. . . .
. . . .
. . . .

b. What is the theme of this passage? Write it down:

. . . .
. . . .
. . . .

c. Does this passage rekindle any memories or experiences? Write them down:

. . . .
. . . .
. . . .

d. What is the Holy Spirit saying to you? Write it down:

. . . .
. . . .
. . . .

4. Read the passage two final times.
   a. Meditate on it.

   b. Is there something God wants you to do with this passage? Is there something He is calling you to? Write it down:

   . . . .
   . . . .
   . . . .

   c. Pray silently. Tell God what this scripture is leading you to think about. Ask Him for His thoughts. Write down your conversation – as if you and God are sitting in a coffee shop, two old and dear friends, sharing:

. . . .

. . . .

. . . .

. . . .

5. Pray and thank God for what He has shared with you. Come back to the passage a few more times over the coming weeks.

My beloved one

My beloved one,

Heaven is not bankrupt and I am not capricious in my giving. I am wholehearted and unchanging in my love for you.

In all of My dealings with you I do seek your growth, an increase in depth and maturity. I stretch out circumstances because I am stretching (increasing) your faith. I am seeking to show you more of how I think and develop you to walk in My paths and know My ways.

Always look to Me. I am the Father who never changes. You are My first fruits to Myself. Everything I do with and for you is by the truth and the exercise of My will.

Live the same as I do. Love the truth and see the will as the primary vehicle for receptivity. Do not allow your emotions to run the show because they will agitate against faith. Your will co-operates with faith and waits patiently for the promise to be fulfilled.

You were called for the very purpose that you might inherit a blessing. The blessing depends upon your positioning before Me. In all things I am teaching you how to be God conscious in all your ways. Developing your will in submission to Mine increases your stability, enlarges your power and enhances your faith.

There is a difference between being slow and being patient. Your Father is not slow but patiently waits for the right time and the right growth.

As you learn to receive My promises, know that I am wanting you to learn much more than how to obtain things. I am teaching you about position, using the will, learning patience and being stretched.

It is through faith *and* patience that you will inherit the promises. I am wholehearted to you *within* the process that I have designated for you in your current circumstances.

The process is the path. Follow it and find Me. I am not far from you. Walk in the manner I am teaching you. All things, always work in your favor. Favor can be immediate or eventual according to the time frame that I have set for you in this current phase.

Relax. Rest in Me. I know what is best. Learn the process of how I want to give to you in this current season. Then everything will come to you and all things will fall to you, as I have decreed.

Your Loving Father

notes

crafted prayer assignment

Use Psalm 25:1–5 as a foundation for mediation.

Write your own version of a crafted prayer that fits
your current situation and what you are learning about
the *Language of Promise*.

FAQ:

frequently asked questions

Q. *Who is Graham Cooke and how can I find more
information about him?*

A. Graham is a speaker and author who lives in
Vacaville, California. He has been involved in
prophetic ministry since 1974. He has developed a
series of training programs on prophecy; leadership;
spirituality; devotional life; walking in the Spirit;
and spiritual warfare. All of which have received
international acclaim for their depth of insight,
revelation and wisdom.

Graham serves on the leadership team of The
Mission in Vacaville where he is part of a think
tank exploring the future and developing strategies
for onward momentum and progression.

You can learn more about Graham at
www.grahamcooke.com.

Q. *How can I become a prayer partner with Graham?*

A. Check his website, www.grahamcooke.com, for all
of the information you need.

Q. *Has Graham written any other books?*

A. To date Graham has written 4 books; co-authored 1 more and written 8 Interactive Journals. These are:

Books:

➢ Developing Your Prophetic Gifting (now out of print).

➢ A Divine Confrontation ... Birth Pangs of the New Church.

➢ Approaching the Heart of Prophecy [Volume 1, Prophetic Series].

➢ Prophecy & Responsibility [Volume 2, Prophetic Series].

Journals:

➢ Hiddenness & Manifestation [Book 1, Being with God Series].

➢ Crafted Prayer [Book 2, Being with God Series].

➢ The Nature of God [Book 3, Being with God Series].

➢ Beholding and Becoming [Book 4, Being with God Series].

➢ Towards a Powerful Inner Life [Book 5, Being with God Series].

- ➤ The Language of Promise [Book 6, Being with God Series].
- ➤ Living in Dependency and Wonder [Book 7, Being with God Series].
- ➤ God's Keeping Power [Book 8, Being with God Series].
- ➤ Qualities of a Spiritual Warrior [Volume 1, The Way of the Warrior Series].
- ➤ Manifesting Your Spirit [Volume 2, The Way of the Warrior Series].

Co-author:
- ➤ Permission Granted with Gary Goodell

You can purchase all of Graham's Full Length Books, Interactive Journals, CDs, DVDs, MP3s,
and E-Books from Graham's publishing company Brilliant Book House by visiting:

www.BrilliantBookHouse.com

About the Author

Graham Cooke is part of The Mission core leadership team, working with senior team leader, David Crone, in Vacaville, California. Graham's role includes training, consulting, mentoring, and being part of a think tank to examine the journey from present to future.

He is married to Theresa who has a passion for worship and dance. She loves to be involved in intercession, warfare, and setting people free. She cares about injustice, abuse, and has compassion on people who are sick, suffering, and disenfranchised.

They have six children and one grandchild. Ben and Seth [32 and 30] both reside and work in the UK. Ben is developing as a writer, is very funny, and probably knows every movie ever made. Seth is a musician, a deep thinker with a caring outlook and amazing capacity for mischief.

Sophie, and son-in-law Mark, live in Vacaville and attend The Mission. Sophie is the Pastoral Assistant for The Mission and Graham's ministry FTI. Sophie has played a significant part in Graham's ministry for a number of years, and has helped develop resources, new books and journals, as well as organize events. Mark and Sophie are a warm-hearted, friendly, deeply humorous couple with lots of friends. Their daughter, Evelyn (August 2006) is a delight — a happy little soul who likes music, loves to dance, and enjoys books.

Daughters Alexis and Alyssa live in Sacramento. Alexis is loving, kind and gentle. She is very intuitive and steadfast toward her friends. Alyssa is a very focused and determines young woman who is fun loving with a witty sense of humor.

Also, Graham and Theresa have two beautiful young women, Julianne and Megan, both in Australia, who are a part of their extended family.

Graham is a popular conference speaker and is well known for his training programs on the prophetic, spiritual warfare, intimacy and devotional life, leadership, spirituality, and the church in transition. He functions as a consultant and free thinker to businesses, churches, and organizations, enabling them to develop strategically. He has a passion to establish the Kingdom and build prototype churches that can fully reach a post-modern society.

A strong part of Graham's ministry is in producing finances and resources to the poor and disenfranchised in developing countries. He supports many projects specifically for widows, orphans, and people in the penal system. He hates abuse of women and works actively against human trafficking and the sex slave trade, including women caught up in prostitution and pornography.

If you would like to invite Graham to minister at an event, please complete our online Ministry Invitation Form at www.grahamcooke.com.

If you wish to become a financial partner for the sake of missions and compassionate acts across the nations, please contact his office at office@grahamcooke.com where his administrative assistant, Jenny Percey, will be happy to assist you.

Graham has many prayer partners who play a significant part in supporting his ministry through intercession and sponsorship. Prayer partners have the honor to be Graham's shield. They are his defensive covering that allows him to advance the Kingdom all over the world. The partners are a vital part of Graham's interdependent team. If you are interested in becoming a prayer partner, please contact his international coordinator, Pam Jarvis, at prayer@grahamcooke.com.

You may contact Graham by writing to:

Graham Cooke
6391 Leisure Town Road
Vacaville, California
95687, USA
www.GrahamCooke.com

About the Author

Criswell Freeman is a Doctor of Clinical Psychology living in Nashville, Tennessee. He is the author of *When Life Throws You a Curveball, Hit It* and *The Wisdom Series* from WALNUT GROVE PRESS. He is also the host of a daily syndicated radio program, *Wisdom Made in America,* which airs in over 300 markets.

About Wisdom Books

Wisdom Books chronicle memorable quotations in an easy-to-read style. Written by Criswell Freeman, this series provides inspiring, thoughtful and humorous messages from entertainers, athletes, scientists, politicians, clerics, writers and renegades. Each title focuses on a particular region or special interest.

Combining his passion for quotations with extensive training in psychology, Dr. Freeman revisits timeless themes such as perseverance, courage, love, forgiveness and faith.

"Quotations help us remember the simple yet profound truths that give life perspective and meaning," notes Freeman. "When it comes to life's most important lessons, we can all use gentle reminders."

The Wisdom Series
by Dr. Criswell Freeman

Wisdom Made In America
ISBN 1-887655-07-7

The Book of Southern Wisdom
ISBN 0-9640955-3-X

The Wisdom of the Midwest
ISBN 1-887655-17-4

The Book of Texas Wisdom
ISBN 0-9640955-8-0

The Book of Florida Wisdom
ISBN 0-9640955-9-9

The Book of California Wisdom
ISBN 1-887655-14-X

The of Book New England Wisdom
ISBN 1-887655-15-8

The Book of New York Wisdom
ISBN 1-887655-16-6

The Book of Country Music Wisdom
ISBN 0-9640955-1-3

The Wisdom of Old-Time Television
ISBN 1-887655-64-6

The Golfer's Book of Wisdom
ISBN 0-9640955-6-4

The Wisdom of Southern Football
ISBN 0-9640955-7-2

The Book of Stock Car Wisdom
ISBN 1-887655-12-3

The Wisdom of Old-Time Baseball
ISBN 1-887655-13-1

The Book of Football Wisdom
ISBN 1-887655-18-2

Wisdom Books are available through booksellers everywhere.
For information about a retailer near you, call 1-800-256-8584.